Restaurant _____ [

Server name _____

MW00887213

Party member	Meal ordered	Quality	Price
		Total	

--- **Server** ---

Warm welcome? _____

Attentiveness and pace of service _____

Gave good recommendations? _____

Accuracy of service _____

--- **Beverage Service** ---

Good recommendations? _____ Checked ID? _____

Experience? _____ Quality of drinks _____

--- **Restaurant** ---

Restaurant cleanliness _____

Restroom cleanliness _____

--- **Overall Impressions** ---

Would you recommend this restaurant? _____

Opportunities for improvement _____

Mileage _____ Compensation _____ Received _____

Restaurant _____ Date of visit _____ Time _____

Server name _____ Manager on duty _____

Party member	Meal ordered	Quality	Price
		Total	

Server

Warm welcome? _____

Attentiveness and pace of service _____

Gave good recommendations? _____

Accuracy of service _____

Beverage Service

Good recommendations? _____ Checked ID? _____

Experience? _____ Quality of drinks _____

Restaurant

Restaurant cleanliness _____

Restroom cleanliness _____

Overall Impressions

Would you recommend this restaurant? _____

Opportunities for improvement _____

Mileage _____ Compensation _____ Received _____

Restaurant _____ Date of visit _____ Time _____

Server name _____ Manager on duty _____

Party member	Meal ordered	Quality	Price
		Total	

Server

Warm welcome?	_____
Attentiveness and pace of service	_____
Gave good recommendations?	_____
Accuracy of service	_____

Beverage Service

Good recommendations?	_____	Checked ID?	_____
Experience?	_____	Quality of drinks	_____

Restaurant

Restaurant cleanliness	_____
Restroom cleanliness	_____

Overall Impressions

Would you recommend this restaurant?	_____
Opportunities for improvement	_____

Mileage _____ Compensation _____ Received _____

Restaurant _____ Date of visit _____ Time _____

Server name _____ Manager on duty _____

Party member	Meal ordered	Quality	Price
		Total	

Server

Warm welcome? _____

Attentiveness and pace of service _____

Gave good recommendations? _____

Accuracy of service _____

Beverage Service

Good recommendations? _____ Checked ID? _____

Experience? _____ Quality of drinks _____

Restaurant

Restaurant cleanliness _____

Restroom cleanliness _____

Overall Impressions

Would you recommend this restaurant? _____

Opportunities for improvement _____

Mileage _____ Compensation _____ Received _____

Restaurant _____ Date of visit _____ Time _____

Server name _____ Manager on duty _____

Party member	Meal ordered	Quality	Price
		Total	

Server

Warm welcome? _____

Attentiveness and pace of service _____

Gave good recommendations? _____

Accuracy of service _____

Beverage Service

Good recommendations? _____ Checked ID? _____

Experience? _____ Quality of drinks _____

Restaurant

Restaurant cleanliness _____

Restroom cleanliness _____

Overall Impressions

Would you recommend this restaurant? _____

Opportunities for improvement _____

Mileage _____ Compensation _____ Received _____

Restaurant _____ Date of visit _____ Time _____

Server name _____ Manager on duty _____

Party member	Meal ordered	Quality	Price
		Total	

Server

Warm welcome? _____

Attentiveness and pace of service _____

Gave good recommendations? _____

Accuracy of service _____

Beverage Service

Good recommendations? _____ Checked ID? _____

Experience? _____ Quality of drinks _____

Restaurant

Restaurant cleanliness _____

Restroom cleanliness _____

Overall Impressions

Would you recommend this restaurant? _____

Opportunities for improvement _____

Mileage _____ Compensation _____ Received _____

Restaurant _____ Date of visit _____ Time _____

Server name _____ Manager on duty _____

Party member	Meal ordered	Quality	Price
		Total	

┌─ **Server** ─────────────────────────────────┐

Warm welcome? _____

Attentiveness and pace of service _____

Gave good recommendations? _____

Accuracy of service _____

└──┘

┌─ **Beverage Service** ───────────────────────┐

Good recommendations? _____ Checked ID? _____

Experience? _____ Quality of drinks

└──┘

┌─ **Restaurant** ─────────────────────────────┐

Restaurant cleanliness _____

Restroom cleanliness _____

└──┘

┌─ **Overall Impressions** ────────────────────┐

Would you recommend this restaurant? _____

Opportunities for improvement _____

└──┘

Mileage _____ Compensation _____ Received _____

Restaurant _____ Date of visit _____ Time _____

Server name _____ Manager on duty _____

Party member	Meal ordered	Quality	Price
		Total	

┌─ **Server** ─────────────────────────────────┐

Warm welcome? _____

Attentiveness and pace of service _____

Gave good recommendations? _____

Accuracy of service _____

└──┘

┌─ **Beverage Service** ───────────────────────┐

Good recommendations? _____ Checked ID? _____

Experience? _____ Quality of drinks _____

└──┘

┌─ **Restaurant** ─────────────────────────────┐

Restaurant cleanliness _____

Restroom cleanliness _____

└──┘

┌─ **Overall Impressions** ────────────────────┐

Would you recommend this restaurant? _____

Opportunities for improvement _____

└──┘

Mileage _____ Compensation _____ Received _____

Restaurant _____ Date of visit _____ Time _____

Server name _____ Manager on duty _____

Party member	Meal ordered	Quality	Price
		Total	

Server

Warm welcome? _____

Attentiveness and pace of service _____

Gave good recommendations? _____

Accuracy of service _____

Beverage Service

Good recommendations? _____ Checked ID? _____

Experience? _____ Quality of drinks _____

Restaurant

Restaurant cleanliness _____

Restroom cleanliness _____

Overall Impressions

Would you recommend this restaurant? _____

Opportunities for improvement _____

Mileage _____ Compensation _____ Received _____

Restaurant _____ Date of visit _____ Time _____

Server name _____ Manager on duty _____

Party member	Meal ordered	Quality	Price
		Total	

Server

Warm welcome? _____

Attentiveness and pace of service _____

Gave good recommendations? _____

Accuracy of service _____

Beverage Service

Good recommendations? _____ Checked ID? _____

Experience? _____ Quality of drinks _____

Restaurant

Restaurant cleanliness _____

Restroom cleanliness _____

Overall Impressions

Would you recommend this restaurant? _____

Opportunities for improvement _____

Mileage _____ Compensation _____ Received _____

Restaurant _____ Date of visit _____ Time _____

Server name _____ Manager on duty _____

Party member	Meal ordered	Quality	Price
		Total	

Server

Warm welcome? _____

Attentiveness and pace of service _____

Gave good recommendations? _____

Accuracy of service _____

Beverage Service

Good recommendations? _____ Checked ID? _____

Experience? _____ Quality of drinks _____

Restaurant

Restaurant cleanliness _____

Restroom cleanliness _____

Overall Impressions

Would you recommend this restaurant? _____

Opportunities for improvement _____

Mileage _____ Compensation _____ Received _____

Restaurant _____ Date of visit _____ Time _____

Server name _____ Manager on duty _____

Party member	Meal ordered	Quality	Price
		Total	

Server

Warm welcome? _____

Attentiveness and pace of service _____

Gave good recommendations? _____

Accuracy of service _____

Beverage Service

Good recommendations? _____ Checked ID? _____

Experience? _____ Quality of drinks _____

Restaurant

Restaurant cleanliness _____

Restroom cleanliness _____

Overall Impressions

Would you recommend this restaurant? _____

Opportunities for improvement _____

Mileage _____ Compensation _____ Received _____

Restaurant _____ Date of visit _____ Time _____

Server name _____ Manager on duty _____

Party member	Meal ordered	Quality	Price
		Total	

Server

Warm welcome? _____

Attentiveness and pace of service _____

Gave good recommendations? _____

Accuracy of service _____

Beverage Service

Good recommendations? _____ Checked ID? _____

Experience? _____ Quality of drinks _____

Restaurant

Restaurant cleanliness _____

Restroom cleanliness _____

Overall Impressions

Would you recommend this restaurant? _____

Opportunities for improvement _____

Mileage _____ Compensation _____ Received _____

Restaurant _____ Date of visit _____ Time _____

Server name _____ Manager on duty _____

Party member	Meal ordered	Quality	Price
		Total	

Server

Warm welcome? _____

Attentiveness and pace of service _____

Gave good recommendations? _____

Accuracy of service _____

Beverage Service

Good recommendations? _____ Checked ID? _____

Experience? _____ Quality of drinks _____

Restaurant

Restaurant cleanliness _____

Restroom cleanliness _____

Overall Impressions

Would you recommend this restaurant? _____

Opportunities for improvement _____

Mileage _____ Compensation _____ Received _____

Restaurant _____ Date of visit _____ Time _____

Server name _____ Manager on duty _____

Party member	Meal ordered	Quality	Price
		Total	

Server

Warm welcome? _____

Attentiveness and pace of service _____

Gave good recommendations? _____

Accuracy of service _____

Beverage Service

Good recommendations? _____ Checked ID? _____

Experience? _____ Quality of drinks _____

Restaurant

Restaurant cleanliness _____

Restroom cleanliness _____

Overall Impressions

Would you recommend this restaurant? _____

Opportunities for improvement _____

Mileage _____ Compensation _____ Received _____

Restaurant _____ Date of visit _____ Time _____

Server name _____ Manager on duty _____

Party member	Meal ordered	Quality	Price
		Total	

Server

Warm welcome? _____

Attentiveness and pace of service _____

Gave good recommendations? _____

Accuracy of service _____

Beverage Service

Good recommendations? _____ Checked ID? _____

Experience? _____ Quality of drinks _____

Restaurant

Restaurant cleanliness _____

Restroom cleanliness _____

Overall Impressions

Would you recommend this restaurant? _____

Opportunities for improvement _____

Mileage _____ Compensation _____ Received _____

Restaurant _____ Date of visit _____ Time _____

Server name _____ Manager on duty _____

Party member	Meal ordered	Quality	Price
		Total	

Server

Warm welcome? _____

Attentiveness and pace of service _____

Gave good recommendations? _____

Accuracy of service _____

Beverage Service

Good recommendations? _____ Checked ID? _____

Experience? _____ Quality of drinks _____

Restaurant

Restaurant cleanliness _____

Restroom cleanliness _____

Overall Impressions

Would you recommend this restaurant? _____

Opportunities for improvement _____

Mileage _____ Compensation _____ Received _____

Restaurant _____ Date of visit _____ Time _____

Server name _____ Manager on duty _____

Party member	Meal ordered	Quality	Price
		Total	

Server

Warm welcome? _____

Attentiveness and pace of service _____

Gave good recommendations? _____

Accuracy of service _____

Beverage Service

Good recommendations? _____   Checked ID? _____

Experience? _____   Quality of drinks _____

Restaurant

Restaurant cleanliness _____

Restroom cleanliness _____

Overall Impressions

Would you recommend this restaurant? _____

Opportunities for improvement _____

Mileage _____   Compensation _____   Received _____

Restaurant _____ Date of visit _____ Time _____

Server name _____ Manager on duty _____

Party member	Meal ordered	Quality	Price
		Total	

Server

Warm welcome? _____

Attentiveness and pace of service _____

Gave good recommendations? _____

Accuracy of service _____

Beverage Service

Good recommendations? _____ Checked ID? _____

Experience? _____ Quality of drinks _____

Restaurant

Restaurant cleanliness _____

Restroom cleanliness _____

Overall Impressions

Would you recommend this restaurant? _____

Opportunities for improvement _____

Mileage _____ Compensation _____ Received _____

Restaurant _____ Date of visit _____ Time _____

Server name _____ Manager on duty _____

Party member	Meal ordered	Quality	Price
		Total	

Server

Warm welcome? _____

Attentiveness and pace of service _____

Gave good recommendations? _____

Accuracy of service _____

Beverage Service

Good recommendations? _____   Checked ID? _____

Experience? _____   Quality of drinks _____

Restaurant

Restaurant cleanliness _____

Restroom cleanliness _____

Overall Impressions

Would you recommend this restaurant? _____

Opportunities for improvement _____

Mileage _____   Compensation _____   Received _____

Restaurant _____ Date of visit _____ Time _____

Server name _____ Manager on duty _____

Party member	Meal ordered	Quality	Price
		Total	

Server

Warm welcome? _____

Attentiveness and pace of service _____

Gave good recommendations? _____

Accuracy of service _____

Beverage Service

Good recommendations? _____ Checked ID? _____

Experience? _____ Quality of drinks

Restaurant

Restaurant cleanliness _____

Restroom cleanliness _____

Overall Impressions

Would you recommend this restaurant? _____

Opportunities for improvement _____

Mileage _____ Compensation _____ Received _____

Restaurant _____ Date of visit _____ Time _____

Server name _____ Manager on duty _____

Party member	Meal ordered	Quality	Price
		Total	

Server

Warm welcome? _____

Attentiveness and pace of service _____

Gave good recommendations? _____

Accuracy of service _____

Beverage Service

Good recommendations? _____ Checked ID? _____

Experience? _____ Quality of drinks _____

Restaurant

Restaurant cleanliness _____

Restroom cleanliness _____

Overall Impressions

Would you recommend this restaurant? _____

Opportunities for improvement _____

Mileage _____ Compensation _____ Received _____

Restaurant _____ Date of visit _____ Time _____

Server name _____ Manager on duty _____

Party member	Meal ordered	Quality	Price
		Total	

Server

Warm welcome? _____

Attentiveness and pace of service _____

Gave good recommendations? _____

Accuracy of service _____

Beverage Service

Good recommendations? _____ Checked ID? _____

Experience? _____ Quality of drinks _____

Restaurant

Restaurant cleanliness _____

Restroom cleanliness _____

Overall Impressions

Would you recommend this restaurant? _____

Opportunities for improvement _____

Mileage _____ Compensation _____ Received _____

Restaurant _____ Date of visit _____ Time _____

Server name _____ Manager on duty _____

Party member	Meal ordered	Quality	Price
		Total	

Server

Warm welcome? _____

Attentiveness and pace of service _____

Gave good recommendations? _____

Accuracy of service _____

Beverage Service

Good recommendations? _____   Checked ID? _____

Experience? _____   Quality of drinks _____

Restaurant

Restaurant cleanliness _____

Restroom cleanliness _____

Overall Impressions

Would you recommend this restaurant? _____

Opportunities for improvement _____

Mileage _____ Compensation _____ Received _____

Restaurant _____   Date of visit _____   Time _____

Server name _____   Manager on duty _____

Party member	Meal ordered	Quality	Price
		Total	

Server

Warm welcome? _____

Attentiveness and pace of service _____

Gave good recommendations? _____

Accuracy of service _____

Beverage Service

Good recommendations? _____   Checked ID? _____

Experience? _____   Quality of drinks _____

Restaurant

Restaurant cleanliness _____

Restroom cleanliness _____

Overall Impressions

Would you recommend this restaurant? _____

Opportunities for improvement _____

Mileage _____   Compensation _____   Received _____

Restaurant _____ Date of visit _____ Time _____

Server name _____ Manager on duty _____

Party member	Meal ordered	Quality	Price
		Total	

Server

Warm welcome? _____

Attentiveness and pace of service _____

Gave good recommendations? _____

Accuracy of service _____

Beverage Service

Good recommendations? _____ Checked ID? _____

Experience? _____ Quality of drinks _____

Restaurant

Restaurant cleanliness _____

Restroom cleanliness _____

Overall Impressions

Would you recommend this restaurant? _____

Opportunities for improvement _____

Mileage _____ Compensation _____ Received _____

Restaurant _____ Date of visit _____ Time _____

Server name _____ Manager on duty _____

Party member	Meal ordered	Quality	Price
		Total	

Server

Warm welcome? _____

Attentiveness and pace of service _____

Gave good recommendations? _____

Accuracy of service _____

Beverage Service

Good recommendations? _____ Checked ID? _____

Experience? _____ Quality of drinks

Restaurant

Restaurant cleanliness _____

Restroom cleanliness _____

Overall Impressions

Would you recommend this restaurant? _____

Opportunities for improvement _____

Mileage _____ Compensation _____ Received _____

Restaurant _____ Date of visit _____ Time _____

Server name _____ Manager on duty _____

Party member	Meal ordered	Quality	Price
		Total	

Server

Warm welcome? _____

Attentiveness and pace of service _____

Gave good recommendations? _____

Accuracy of service _____

Beverage Service

Good recommendations? _____ Checked ID? _____

Experience? _____ Quality of drinks _____

Restaurant

Restaurant cleanliness _____

Restroom cleanliness _____

Overall Impressions

Would you recommend this restaurant? _____

Opportunities for improvement _____

Mileage _____ Compensation _____ Received _____

Restaurant _____ Date of visit _____ Time _____

Server name _____ Manager on duty _____

Party member	Meal ordered	Quality	Price
		Total	

Server

Warm welcome? _____

Attentiveness and pace of service _____

Gave good recommendations? _____

Accuracy of service _____

Beverage Service

Good recommendations? _____   Checked ID? _____

Experience? _____   Quality of drinks _____

Restaurant

Restaurant cleanliness _____

Restroom cleanliness _____

Overall Impressions

Would you recommend this restaurant? _____

Opportunities for improvement _____

Mileage _____   Compensation _____   Received _____

Restaurant _____ Date of visit _____ Time _____

Server name _____ Manager on duty _____

Party member	Meal ordered	Quality	Price
		Total	

Server

Warm welcome? _____

Attentiveness and pace of service _____

Gave good recommendations? _____

Accuracy of service _____

Beverage Service

Good recommendations? _____   Checked ID? _____

Experience? _____   Quality of drinks _____

Restaurant

Restaurant cleanliness _____

Restroom cleanliness _____

Overall Impressions

Would you recommend this restaurant? _____

Opportunities for improvement _____

Mileage _____ Compensation _____ Received _____

Restaurant _____ Date of visit _____ Time _____

Server name _____ Manager on duty _____

Party member	Meal ordered	Quality	Price
		Total	

┌─ **Server** ─────────────────────────
│ Warm welcome? _____
│ Attentiveness and pace of service _____
│ Gave good recommendations? _____
│ Accuracy of service _____

┌─ **Beverage Service** ─────────────────
│ Good recommendations? _____ Checked ID? _____
│ Experience? _____ Quality of drinks _____

┌─ **Restaurant** ─────────────────────
│ Restaurant cleanliness _____
│ Restroom cleanliness _____

┌─ **Overall Impressions** ─────────────
│ Would you recommend this restaurant? _____
│ Opportunities for improvement _____

Mileage _____ Compensation _____ Received _____

Restaurant _____ Date of visit _____ Time _____

Server name _____ Manager on duty _____

Party member	Meal ordered	Quality	Price
		Total	

Server

Warm welcome? _____

Attentiveness and pace of service _____

Gave good recommendations? _____

Accuracy of service _____

Beverage Service

Good recommendations? _____ Checked ID? _____

Experience? _____ Quality of drinks _____

Restaurant

Restaurant cleanliness _____

Restroom cleanliness _____

Overall Impressions

Would you recommend this restaurant? _____

Opportunities for improvement _____

Mileage _____ Compensation _____ Received _____

Restaurant _____ Date of visit _____ Time _____

Server name _____ Manager on duty _____

Party member	Meal ordered	Quality	Price
		Total	

Server

Warm welcome? _____

Attentiveness and pace of service _____

Gave good recommendations? _____

Accuracy of service _____

Beverage Service

Good recommendations? _____   Checked ID? _____

Experience? _____   Quality of drinks _____

Restaurant

Restaurant cleanliness _____

Restroom cleanliness _____

Overall Impressions

Would you recommend this restaurant? _____

Opportunities for improvement _____

Mileage _____   Compensation _____   Received _____

Restaurant _____ Date of visit _____ Time _____

Server name _____ Manager on duty _____

Party member	Meal ordered	Quality	Price
		Total	

Server

Warm welcome? _____

Attentiveness and pace of service _____

Gave good recommendations? _____

Accuracy of service _____

Beverage Service

Good recommendations? _____   Checked ID? _____

Experience? _____   Quality of drinks _____

Restaurant

Restaurant cleanliness _____

Restroom cleanliness _____

Overall Impressions

Would you recommend this restaurant? _____

Opportunities for improvement _____

Mileage _____ Compensation _____ Received _____

Restaurant _____ Date of visit _____ Time _____

Server name _____ Manager on duty _____

Party member	Meal ordered	Quality	Price
	Total		

Server

Warm welcome? _____

Attentiveness and pace of service _____

Gave good recommendations? _____

Accuracy of service _____

Beverage Service

Good recommendations? _____   Checked ID? _____

Experience? _____   Quality of drinks _____

Restaurant

Restaurant cleanliness _____

Restroom cleanliness _____

Overall Impressions

Would you recommend this restaurant? _____

Opportunities for improvement _____

Mileage _____   Compensation _____   Received _____

Restaurant _____ Date of visit _____ Time _____

Server name _____ Manager on duty _____

Party member	Meal ordered	Quality	Price
		Total	

Server

Warm welcome? _____

Attentiveness and pace of service _____

Gave good recommendations? _____

Accuracy of service _____

Beverage Service

Good recommendations? _____ Checked ID? _____

Experience? _____ Quality of drinks _____

Restaurant

Restaurant cleanliness _____

Restroom cleanliness _____

Overall Impressions

Would you recommend this restaurant? _____

Opportunities for improvement _____

Mileage _____ Compensation _____ Received _____

Restaurant _____ Date of visit _____ Time _____

Server name _____ Manager on duty _____

Party member	Meal ordered	Quality	Price
		Total	

Server

Warm welcome? _____

Attentiveness and pace of service _____

Gave good recommendations? _____

Accuracy of service _____

Beverage Service

Good recommendations? _____ Checked ID? _____

Experience? _____ Quality of drinks _____

Restaurant

Restaurant cleanliness _____

Restroom cleanliness _____

Overall Impressions

Would you recommend this restaurant? _____

Opportunities for improvement _____

Mileage _____ Compensation _____ Received _____

Restaurant _____ Date of visit _____ Time _____

Server name _____ Manager on duty _____

Party member	Meal ordered	Quality	Price
		Total	

Server

Warm welcome? _____

Attentiveness and pace of service _____

Gave good recommendations? _____

Accuracy of service _____

Beverage Service

Good recommendations? _____ Checked ID? _____

Experience? _____ Quality of drinks _____

Restaurant

Restaurant cleanliness _____

Restroom cleanliness _____

Overall Impressions

Would you recommend this restaurant? _____

Opportunities for improvement _____

Mileage _____ Compensation _____ Received _____

Restaurant _____ Date of visit _____ Time _____

Server name _____ Manager on duty _____

Party member	Meal ordered	Quality	Price
		Total	

Server

Warm welcome? _____

Attentiveness and pace of service _____

Gave good recommendations? _____

Accuracy of service _____

Beverage Service

Good recommendations? _____ Checked ID? _____

Experience? _____ Quality of drinks _____

Restaurant

Restaurant cleanliness _____

Restroom cleanliness _____

Overall Impressions

Would you recommend this restaurant? _____

Opportunities for improvement _____

Mileage _____ Compensation _____ Received _____

Restaurant _____ Date of visit _____ Time _____

Server name _____ Manager on duty _____

Party member	Meal ordered	Quality	Price
		Total	

Server

Warm welcome? _____

Attentiveness and pace of service _____

Gave good recommendations? _____

Accuracy of service _____

Beverage Service

Good recommendations? _____   Checked ID? _____

Experience? _____   Quality of drinks _____

Restaurant

Restaurant cleanliness _____

Restroom cleanliness _____

Overall Impressions

Would you recommend this restaurant? _____

Opportunities for improvement _____

Mileage _____   Compensation _____   Received _____

Restaurant _____ Date of visit _____ Time _____

Server name _____ Manager on duty _____

Party member	Meal ordered	Quality	Price
		Total	

Server

Warm welcome? _____

Attentiveness and pace of service _____

Gave good recommendations? _____

Accuracy of service _____

Beverage Service

Good recommendations? _____ Checked ID? _____

Experience? _____ Quality of drinks _____

Restaurant

Restaurant cleanliness _____

Restroom cleanliness _____

Overall Impressions

Would you recommend this restaurant? _____

Opportunities for improvement _____

Mileage _____ Compensation _____ Received _____

| Restaurant | _____ | Date of visit _____ | Time _____ |

Server name _____   Manager on duty _____

Party member	Meal ordered	Quality	Price
		Total	

Server

Warm welcome? _____

Attentiveness and pace of service _____

Gave good recommendations? _____

Accuracy of service _____

Beverage Service

Good recommendations? _____   Checked ID? _____

Experience? _____   Quality of drinks _____

Restaurant

Restaurant cleanliness _____

Restroom cleanliness _____

Overall Impressions

Would you recommend this restaurant? _____

Opportunities for improvement _____

Mileage _____   Compensation _____   Received _____

Restaurant _____ Date of visit _____ Time _____

Server name _____ Manager on duty _____

Party member	Meal ordered	Quality	Price
		Total	

Server

Warm welcome? _____

Attentiveness and pace of service _____

Gave good recommendations? _____

Accuracy of service _____

Beverage Service

Good recommendations? _____ Checked ID? _____

Experience? _____ Quality of drinks

Restaurant

Restaurant cleanliness _____

Restroom cleanliness _____

Overall Impressions

Would you recommend this restaurant? _____

Opportunities for improvement _____

Mileage _____ Compensation _____ Received _____

Restaurant _____ Date of visit _____ Time _____

Server name _____ Manager on duty _____

Party member	Meal ordered	Quality	Price
		Total	

Server

Warm welcome? _____

Attentiveness and pace of service _____

Gave good recommendations? _____

Accuracy of service _____

Beverage Service

Good recommendations? _____ Checked ID? _____

Experience? _____ Quality of drinks _____

Restaurant

Restaurant cleanliness _____

Restroom cleanliness _____

Overall Impressions

Would you recommend this restaurant? _____

Opportunities for improvement _____

Mileage _____ Compensation _____ Received _____

Restaurant _____ Date of visit _____ Time _____

Server name _____ Manager on duty _____

Party member	Meal ordered	Quality	Price
		Total	

Server

Warm welcome? _____

Attentiveness and pace of service _____

Gave good recommendations? _____

Accuracy of service _____

Beverage Service

Good recommendations? _____ Checked ID? _____

Experience? _____ Quality of drinks _____

Restaurant

Restaurant cleanliness _____

Restroom cleanliness _____

Overall Impressions

Would you recommend this restaurant? _____

Opportunities for improvement _____

Mileage _____ Compensation _____ Received _____

Restaurant _____   Date of visit _____   Time _____

Server name _____   Manager on duty _____

Party member	Meal ordered	Quality	Price
		Total	

Server

Warm welcome? _____

Attentiveness and pace of service _____

Gave good recommendations? _____

Accuracy of service _____

Beverage Service

Good recommendations? _____   Checked ID? _____

Experience? _____   Quality of drinks _____

Restaurant

Restaurant cleanliness _____

Restroom cleanliness _____

Overall Impressions

Would you recommend this restaurant? _____

Opportunities for improvement _____

Mileage _____   Compensation _____   Received _____

Restaurant _____ Date of visit _____ Time _____

Server name _____ Manager on duty _____

Party member	Meal ordered	Quality	Price
		Total	

┌─ **Server** ─────────────────────────────┐

Warm welcome? _____

Attentiveness and pace of service _____

Gave good recommendations? _____

Accuracy of service _____

└──┘

┌─ **Beverage Service** ───────────────────┐

Good recommendations? _____ Checked ID? _____

Experience? _____ Quality of drinks _____

└──┘

┌─ **Restaurant** ─────────────────────────┐

Restaurant cleanliness _____

Restroom cleanliness _____

└──┘

┌─ **Overall Impressions** ────────────────┐

Would you recommend this restaurant? _____

Opportunities for improvement _____

└──┘

Mileage _____ Compensation _____ Received _____

Restaurant _____ Date of visit _____ Time _____

Server name _____ Manager on duty _____

Party member	Meal ordered	Quality	Price
		Total	

Server

Warm welcome? _____

Attentiveness and pace of service _____

Gave good recommendations? _____

Accuracy of service _____

Beverage Service

Good recommendations? _____   Checked ID? _____

Experience? _____   Quality of drinks _____

Restaurant

Restaurant cleanliness _____

Restroom cleanliness _____

Overall Impressions

Would you recommend this restaurant? _____

Opportunities for improvement _____

Mileage _____   Compensation _____   Received _____

Restaurant _____   Date of visit _____   Time _____

Server name _____   Manager on duty _____

Party member	Meal ordered	Quality	Price
		Total	

┌─ **Server** ──────────────────────────┐

Warm welcome? _____

Attentiveness and pace of service _____

Gave good recommendations? _____

Accuracy of service _____

└──────────────────────────────────────┘

┌─ **Beverage Service** ─────────────────┐

Good recommendations? _____   Checked ID? _____

Experience? _____   Quality of drinks _____

└──────────────────────────────────────┘

┌─ **Restaurant** ──────────────────────┐

Restaurant cleanliness _____

Restroom cleanliness _____

└──────────────────────────────────────┘

┌─ **Overall Impressions** ──────────────┐

Would you recommend this restaurant? _____

Opportunities for improvement _____

└──────────────────────────────────────┘

Mileage _____   Compensation _____   Received _____

Restaurant _____ Date of visit _____ Time _____

Server name _____ Manager on duty _____

Party member	Meal ordered	Quality	Price
		Total	

Server

Warm welcome? _____

Attentiveness and pace of service _____

Gave good recommendations? _____

Accuracy of service _____

Beverage Service

Good recommendations? _____   Checked ID? _____

Experience? _____   Quality of drinks _____

Restaurant

Restaurant cleanliness _____

Restroom cleanliness _____

Overall Impressions

Would you recommend this restaurant? _____

Opportunities for improvement _____

Mileage _____   Compensation _____   Received _____

Restaurant _____ Date of visit _____ Time _____

Server name _____ Manager on duty _____

Party member	Meal ordered	Quality	Price
		Total	

Server

Warm welcome? _____

Attentiveness and pace of service _____

Gave good recommendations? _____

Accuracy of service _____

Beverage Service

Good recommendations? _____ Checked ID? _____

Experience? _____ Quality of drinks _____

Restaurant

Restaurant cleanliness _____

Restroom cleanliness _____

Overall Impressions

Would you recommend this restaurant? _____

Opportunities for improvement _____

Mileage _____ Compensation _____ Received _____

Restaurant _____ Date of visit _____ Time _____

Server name _____ Manager on duty _____

Party member	Meal ordered	Quality	Price
		Total	

Server

Warm welcome? _____

Attentiveness and pace of service _____

Gave good recommendations? _____

Accuracy of service _____

Beverage Service

Good recommendations? _____ Checked ID? _____

Experience? _____ Quality of drinks _____

Restaurant

Restaurant cleanliness _____

Restroom cleanliness _____

Overall Impressions

Would you recommend this restaurant? _____

Opportunities for improvement _____

Mileage _____ Compensation _____ Received _____

Restaurant _____ Date of visit _____ Time _____

Server name _____ Manager on duty _____

Party member	Meal ordered	Quality	Price
		Total	

Server

Warm welcome? _____

Attentiveness and pace of service _____

Gave good recommendations? _____

Accuracy of service _____

Beverage Service

Good recommendations? _____ Checked ID? _____

Experience? _____ Quality of drinks _____

Restaurant

Restaurant cleanliness _____

Restroom cleanliness _____

Overall Impressions

Would you recommend this restaurant? _____

Opportunities for improvement _____

Mileage _____ Compensation _____ Received _____

Restaurant _____ Date of visit _____ Time _____

Server name _____ Manager on duty _____

Party member	Meal ordered	Quality	Price
		Total	

Server

Warm welcome? _____

Attentiveness and pace of service _____

Gave good recommendations? _____

Accuracy of service _____

Beverage Service

Good recommendations? _____ Checked ID? _____

Experience? _____ Quality of drinks _____

Restaurant

Restaurant cleanliness _____

Restroom cleanliness _____

Overall Impressions

Would you recommend this restaurant? _____

Opportunities for improvement _____

Mileage _____ Compensation _____ Received _____

Restaurant _____ Date of visit _____ Time _____

Server name _____ Manager on duty _____

Party member	Meal ordered	Quality	Price
		Total	

Server

Warm welcome? _____

Attentiveness and pace of service _____

Gave good recommendations? _____

Accuracy of service _____

Beverage Service

Good recommendations? _____ Checked ID? _____

Experience? _____ Quality of drinks _____

Restaurant

Restaurant cleanliness _____

Restroom cleanliness _____

Overall Impressions

Would you recommend this restaurant? _____

Opportunities for improvement _____

Mileage _____ Compensation _____ Received _____

Restaurant _____ Date of visit _____ Time _____

Server name _____ Manager on duty _____

Party member	Meal ordered	Quality	Price
		Total	

Server

Warm welcome? _____

Attentiveness and pace of service _____

Gave good recommendations? _____

Accuracy of service _____

Beverage Service

Good recommendations? _____ Checked ID? _____

Experience? _____ Quality of drinks _____

Restaurant

Restaurant cleanliness _____

Restroom cleanliness _____

Overall Impressions

Would you recommend this restaurant? _____

Opportunities for improvement _____

Mileage _____ Compensation _____ Received _____

Restaurant _____ Date of visit _____ Time _____

Server name _____ Manager on duty _____

Party member	Meal ordered	Quality	Price
		Total	

Server

Warm welcome? _____

Attentiveness and pace of service _____

Gave good recommendations? _____

Accuracy of service _____

Beverage Service

Good recommendations? _____ Checked ID? _____

Experience? _____ Quality of drinks _____

Restaurant

Restaurant cleanliness _____

Restroom cleanliness _____

Overall Impressions

Would you recommend this restaurant? _____

Opportunities for improvement _____

Mileage _____ Compensation _____ Received _____

Restaurant _____ Date of visit _____ Time _____

Server name _____ Manager on duty _____

Party member	Meal ordered	Quality	Price
		Total	

Server

Warm welcome? _____

Attentiveness and pace of service _____

Gave good recommendations? _____

Accuracy of service _____

Beverage Service

Good recommendations? _____ Checked ID? _____

Experience? _____ Quality of drinks _____

Restaurant

Restaurant cleanliness _____

Restroom cleanliness _____

Overall Impressions

Would you recommend this restaurant? _____

Opportunities for improvement _____

Mileage _____ Compensation _____ Received _____

Restaurant _____ Date of visit _____ Time _____

Server name _____ Manager on duty _____

Party member	Meal ordered	Quality	Price
		Total	

Server

Warm welcome? _____

Attentiveness and pace of service _____

Gave good recommendations? _____

Accuracy of service _____

Beverage Service

Good recommendations? _____ Checked ID? _____

Experience? _____ Quality of drinks _____

Restaurant

Restaurant cleanliness _____

Restroom cleanliness _____

Overall Impressions

Would you recommend this restaurant? _____

Opportunities for improvement _____

Mileage _____ Compensation _____ Received _____

Restaurant _____ Date of visit _____ Time _____

Server name _____ Manager on duty _____

Party member	Meal ordered	Quality	Price
		Total	

Server

Warm welcome? _____

Attentiveness and pace of service _____

Gave good recommendations? _____

Accuracy of service _____

Beverage Service

Good recommendations? _____   Checked ID? _____

Experience? _____   Quality of drinks _____

Restaurant

Restaurant cleanliness _____

Restroom cleanliness _____

Overall Impressions

Would you recommend this restaurant? _____

Opportunities for improvement _____

Mileage _____ Compensation _____ Received _____

Restaurant _____ Date of visit _____ Time _____

Server name _____ Manager on duty _____

Party member	Meal ordered	Quality	Price
		Total	

Server

Warm welcome? _____

Attentiveness and pace of service _____

Gave good recommendations? _____

Accuracy of service _____

Beverage Service

Good recommendations? _____   Checked ID? _____

Experience? _____   Quality of drinks _____

Restaurant

Restaurant cleanliness _____

Restroom cleanliness _____

Overall Impressions

Would you recommend this restaurant? _____

Opportunities for improvement _____

Mileage _____   Compensation _____   Received _____

Restaurant _____ Date of visit _____ Time _____

Server name _____ Manager on duty _____

Party member	Meal ordered	Quality	Price
		Total	

Server

Warm welcome? _____

Attentiveness and pace of service _____

Gave good recommendations? _____

Accuracy of service _____

Beverage Service

Good recommendations? _____   Checked ID? _____

Experience? _____   Quality of drinks _____

Restaurant

Restaurant cleanliness _____

Restroom cleanliness _____

Overall Impressions

Would you recommend this restaurant? _____

Opportunities for improvement _____

Mileage _____   Compensation _____   Received _____

Restaurant _____ Date of visit _____ Time _____

Server name _____ Manager on duty _____

Party member	Meal ordered	Quality	Price
	Total		

Server

Warm welcome? _____

Attentiveness and pace of service _____

Gave good recommendations? _____

Accuracy of service _____

Beverage Service

Good recommendations? _____ Checked ID? _____

Experience? _____ Quality of drinks _____

Restaurant

Restaurant cleanliness _____

Restroom cleanliness _____

Overall Impressions

Would you recommend this restaurant? _____

Opportunities for improvement _____

Mileage _____ Compensation _____ Received _____

Restaurant _____ Date of visit _____ Time _____

Server name _____ Manager on duty _____

Party member	Meal ordered	Quality	Price
		Total	

Server

Warm welcome? _____

Attentiveness and pace of service _____

Gave good recommendations? _____

Accuracy of service _____

Beverage Service

Good recommendations? _____ Checked ID? _____

Experience? _____ Quality of drinks _____

Restaurant

Restaurant cleanliness _____

Restroom cleanliness _____

Overall Impressions

Would you recommend this restaurant? _____

Opportunities for improvement _____

Mileage _____ Compensation _____ Received _____

Restaurant _____ Date of visit _____ Time _____

Server name _____ Manager on duty _____

Party member	Meal ordered	Quality	Price
		Total	

Server

Warm welcome? _____

Attentiveness and pace of service _____

Gave good recommendations? _____

Accuracy of service _____

Beverage Service

Good recommendations? _____ Checked ID? _____

Experience? _____ Quality of drinks _____

Restaurant

Restaurant cleanliness _____

Restroom cleanliness _____

Overall Impressions

Would you recommend this restaurant? _____

Opportunities for improvement _____

Mileage _____ Compensation _____ Received _____

Restaurant _____ Date of visit _____ Time _____

Server name _____ Manager on duty _____

Party member	Meal ordered	Quality	Price
		Total	

---- **Server** ----

Warm welcome? _____

Attentiveness and pace of service _____

Gave good recommendations? _____

Accuracy of service _____

---- **Beverage Service** ----

Good recommendations? _____ Checked ID? _____

Experience? _____ Quality of drinks _____

---- **Restaurant** ----

Restaurant cleanliness _____

Restroom cleanliness _____

---- **Overall Impressions** ----

Would you recommend this restaurant? _____

Opportunities for improvement _____

Mileage _____ Compensation _____ Received _____

Restaurant _____ Date of visit _____ Time _____

Server name _____ Manager on duty _____

Party member	Meal ordered	Quality	Price
		Total	

Server

Warm welcome? _____

Attentiveness and pace of service _____

Gave good recommendations? _____

Accuracy of service _____

Beverage Service

Good recommendations? _____ Checked ID? _____

Experience? _____ Quality of drinks _____

Restaurant

Restaurant cleanliness _____

Restroom cleanliness _____

Overall Impressions

Would you recommend this restaurant? _____

Opportunities for improvement _____

Mileage _____ Compensation _____ Received _____

Restaurant _____ Date of visit _____ Time _____

Server name _____ Manager on duty _____

Party member	Meal ordered	Quality	Price
		Total	

Server

Warm welcome? _____

Attentiveness and pace of service _____

Gave good recommendations? _____

Accuracy of service _____

Beverage Service

Good recommendations? _____ Checked ID? _____

Experience? _____ Quality of drinks _____

Restaurant

Restaurant cleanliness _____

Restroom cleanliness _____

Overall Impressions

Would you recommend this restaurant? _____

Opportunities for improvement _____

Mileage _____ Compensation _____ Received _____

Restaurant _____ Date of visit _____ Time _____

Server name _____ Manager on duty _____

Party member	Meal ordered	Quality	Price
		Total	

Server

Warm welcome? _____

Attentiveness and pace of service _____

Gave good recommendations? _____

Accuracy of service _____

Beverage Service

Good recommendations? _____   Checked ID? _____

Experience? _____   Quality of drinks _____

Restaurant

Restaurant cleanliness _____

Restroom cleanliness _____

Overall Impressions

Would you recommend this restaurant? _____

Opportunities for improvement _____

Mileage _____ Compensation _____ Received _____

Restaurant _____ Date of visit _____ Time _____

Server name _____ Manager on duty _____

Party member	Meal ordered	Quality	Price
		Total	

Server

Warm welcome? _____

Attentiveness and pace of service _____

Gave good recommendations? _____

Accuracy of service _____

Beverage Service

Good recommendations? _____ Checked ID? _____

Experience? _____ Quality of drinks _____

Restaurant

Restaurant cleanliness _____

Restroom cleanliness _____

Overall Impressions

Would you recommend this restaurant? _____

Opportunities for improvement _____

Mileage _____ Compensation _____ Received _____

Restaurant _____ Date of visit _____ Time _____

Server name _____ Manager on duty _____

Party member	Meal ordered	Quality	Price
		Total	

┌─ **Server** ─────────────────────────────┐

Warm welcome? _____

Attentiveness and pace of service _____

Gave good recommendations? _____

Accuracy of service _____

└──────────────────────────────┘

┌─ **Beverage Service** ─────────────────────┐

Good recommendations? _____ Checked ID? _____

Experience? _____ Quality of drinks _____

└──────────────────────────────┘

┌─ **Restaurant** ─────────────────────────┐

Restaurant cleanliness _____

Restroom cleanliness _____

└──────────────────────────────┘

┌─ **Overall Impressions** ──────────────────┐

Would you recommend this restaurant? _____

Opportunities for improvement _____

└──────────────────────────────┘

Mileage _____ Compensation _____ Received _____

Restaurant _____   Date of visit _____   Time _____

Server name _____   Manager on duty _____

Party member	Meal ordered	Quality	Price
		Total	

Server

Warm welcome? _____

Attentiveness and pace of service _____

Gave good recommendations? _____

Accuracy of service _____

Beverage Service

Good recommendations? _____   Checked ID? _____

Experience? _____   Quality of drinks _____

Restaurant

Restaurant cleanliness _____

Restroom cleanliness _____

Overall Impressions

Would you recommend this restaurant? _____

Opportunities for improvement _____

Mileage _____   Compensation _____   Received _____

Restaurant _____ Date of visit _____ Time _____

Server name _____ Manager on duty _____

Party member	Meal ordered	Quality	Price
	Total		

Server

Warm welcome? _____

Attentiveness and pace of service _____

Gave good recommendations? _____

Accuracy of service _____

Beverage Service

Good recommendations? _____ Checked ID? _____

Experience? _____ Quality of drinks _____

Restaurant

Restaurant cleanliness _____

Restroom cleanliness _____

Overall Impressions

Would you recommend this restaurant? _____

Opportunities for improvement _____

Mileage _____ Compensation _____ Received _____

Restaurant _____ Date of visit _____ Time _____

Server name _____ Manager on duty _____

Party member	Meal ordered	Quality	Price
		Total	

Server

Warm welcome? _____

Attentiveness and pace of service _____

Gave good recommendations? _____

Accuracy of service _____

Beverage Service

Good recommendations? _____   Checked ID? _____

Experience? _____   Quality of drinks _____

Restaurant

Restaurant cleanliness _____

Restroom cleanliness _____

Overall Impressions

Would you recommend this restaurant? _____

Opportunities for improvement _____

Mileage _____   Compensation _____   Received _____

Restaurant _____ Date of visit _____ Time _____

Server name _____ Manager on duty _____

Party member	Meal ordered	Quality	Price
	Total		

Server

Warm welcome? _____

Attentiveness and pace of service _____

Gave good recommendations? _____

Accuracy of service _____

Beverage Service

Good recommendations? _____ Checked ID? _____

Experience? _____ Quality of drinks

Restaurant

Restaurant cleanliness _____

Restroom cleanliness _____

Overall Impressions

Would you recommend this restaurant? _____

Opportunities for improvement _____

Mileage _____ Compensation _____ Received _____

Restaurant _____ Date of visit _____ Time _____

Server name _____ Manager on duty _____

Party member	Meal ordered	Quality	Price
		Total	

Server

Warm welcome? _____

Attentiveness and pace of service _____

Gave good recommendations? _____

Accuracy of service _____

Beverage Service

Good recommendations? _____ Checked ID? _____

Experience? _____ Quality of drinks _____

Restaurant

Restaurant cleanliness _____

Restroom cleanliness _____

Overall Impressions

Would you recommend this restaurant? _____

Opportunities for improvement _____

Mileage _____ Compensation _____ Received _____

Restaurant _____ Date of visit _____ Time _____

Server name _____ Manager on duty _____

Party member	Meal ordered	Quality	Price
		Total	

Server

Warm welcome? _____

Attentiveness and pace of service _____

Gave good recommendations? _____

Accuracy of service _____

Beverage Service

Good recommendations? _____ Checked ID? _____

Experience? _____ Quality of drinks _____

Restaurant

Restaurant cleanliness _____

Restroom cleanliness _____

Overall Impressions

Would you recommend this restaurant? _____

Opportunities for improvement _____

Mileage _____ Compensation _____ Received _____

Restaurant _____ Date of visit _____ Time _____

Server name _____ Manager on duty _____

Party member	Meal ordered	Quality	Price
		Total	

---- **Server** ----

Warm welcome? _____

Attentiveness and pace of service _____

Gave good recommendations? _____

Accuracy of service _____

---- **Beverage Service** ----

Good recommendations? _____ Checked ID? _____

Experience? _____ Quality of drinks _____

---- **Restaurant** ----

Restaurant cleanliness _____

Restroom cleanliness _____

---- **Overall Impressions** ----

Would you recommend this restaurant? _____

Opportunities for improvement _____

Mileage _____ Compensation _____ Received _____

Restaurant _____   Date of visit _____   Time _____

Server name _____   Manager on duty _____

Party member	Meal ordered	Quality	Price
	Total		

Server

Warm welcome? _____

Attentiveness and pace of service _____

Gave good recommendations? _____

Accuracy of service _____

Beverage Service

Good recommendations? _____   Checked ID? _____

Experience? _____   Quality of drinks _____

Restaurant

Restaurant cleanliness _____

Restroom cleanliness _____

Overall Impressions

Would you recommend this restaurant? _____

Opportunities for improvement _____

Mileage _____   Compensation _____   Received _____

Restaurant _____ Date of visit _____ Time _____

Server name _____ Manager on duty _____

Party member	Meal ordered	Quality	Price
		Total	

┌─ **Server** ─────────────────────────────────┐

Warm welcome? _____

Attentiveness and pace of service _____

Gave good recommendations? _____

Accuracy of service _____

└──┘

┌─ **Beverage Service** ───────────────────────┐

Good recommendations? _____ Checked ID? _____

Experience? _____ Quality of drinks _____

└──┘

┌─ **Restaurant** ─────────────────────────────┐

Restaurant cleanliness _____

Restroom cleanliness _____

└──┘

┌─ **Overall Impressions** ────────────────────┐

Would you recommend this restaurant? _____

Opportunities for improvement _____

└──┘

Mileage _____ Compensation _____ Received _____

Restaurant _____ Date of visit _____ Time _____

Server name _____ Manager on duty _____

Party member	Meal ordered	Quality	Price
		Total	

┌─ **Server** ─────────────────────────────┐

Warm welcome? _____

Attentiveness and pace of service _____

Gave good recommendations? _____

Accuracy of service _____

└──┘

┌─ **Beverage Service** ───────────────────┐

Good recommendations? _____ Checked ID? _____

Experience? _____ Quality of drinks _____

└──┘

┌─ **Restaurant** ─────────────────────────┐

Restaurant cleanliness _____

Restroom cleanliness _____

└──┘

┌─ **Overall Impressions** ────────────────┐

Would you recommend this restaurant? _____

Opportunities for improvement _____

└──┘

Mileage _____ Compensation _____ Received _____

Restaurant _____ Date of visit _____ Time _____

Server name _____ Manager on duty _____

Party member	Meal ordered	Quality	Price
		Total	

Server

Warm welcome? _____

Attentiveness and pace of service _____

Gave good recommendations? _____

Accuracy of service _____

Beverage Service

Good recommendations? _____   Checked ID? _____

Experience? _____   Quality of drinks _____

Restaurant

Restaurant cleanliness _____

Restroom cleanliness _____

Overall Impressions

Would you recommend this restaurant? _____

Opportunities for improvement _____

Mileage _____   Compensation _____   Received _____

Restaurant _____ Date of visit _____ Time _____

Server name _____ Manager on duty _____

Party member	Meal ordered	Quality	Price
		Total	

Server

Warm welcome? _____

Attentiveness and pace of service _____

Gave good recommendations? _____

Accuracy of service _____

Beverage Service

Good recommendations? _____ Checked ID? _____

Experience? _____ Quality of drinks _____

Restaurant

Restaurant cleanliness _____

Restroom cleanliness _____

Overall Impressions

Would you recommend this restaurant? _____

Opportunities for improvement _____

Mileage _____ Compensation _____ Received _____

Restaurant _____ Date of visit _____ Time _____

Server name _____ Manager on duty _____

Party member	Meal ordered	Quality	Price
		Total	

Server

Warm welcome? _____

Attentiveness and pace of service _____

Gave good recommendations? _____

Accuracy of service _____

Beverage Service

Good recommendations? _____ Checked ID? _____

Experience? _____ Quality of drinks _____

Restaurant

Restaurant cleanliness _____

Restroom cleanliness _____

Overall Impressions

Would you recommend this restaurant? _____

Opportunities for improvement _____

Mileage _____ Compensation _____ Received _____

Restaurant _____ Date of visit _____ Time _____

Server name _____ Manager on duty _____

Party member	Meal ordered	Quality	Price
		Total	

Server

Warm welcome? _____

Attentiveness and pace of service _____

Gave good recommendations? _____

Accuracy of service _____

Beverage Service

Good recommendations? _____ Checked ID? _____

Experience? _____ Quality of drinks _____

Restaurant

Restaurant cleanliness _____

Restroom cleanliness _____

Overall Impressions

Would you recommend this restaurant? _____

Opportunities for improvement _____

Mileage _____ Compensation _____ Received _____

Made in the USA
Las Vegas, NV
10 February 2021

17585442R00049